The 2016 Guide To Maximizing Your Retirement Income

Joel M. Johnson, CFP®

Printed in The United States of America.

ISBN-13: 978-0692599600
Published by

Big Man Publishing

Table of Contents

Regulatory Issues

Notes To Readers

This publication contains the opinions and ideas of its author. The strategies outlined in this book may not be suitable for every individual and are not guaranteed or warranted to produce any particular results. Presentation of performance data herein does not imply that similar results will be achieved in the future. Any such data are provided merely for illustrative and discussion purposes; rather than focusing on the time periods used or the results derived. The reader should focus instead on the underlying principles.

This book is sold with the understanding that neither publisher nor author, through this book, is engaged in rendering legal, tax, investment, insurance, financial, accounting or other professional advice or services. If the reader requires such advice or services, a competent professional should be consulted. Relevant laws vary from state to state.

No warranty is made with respect to the accuracy or the completeness of the information contained herein, and both the author and the publisher specifically disclaim any responsibility for any liability, loss, or risk, personal or otherwise, that is incurred as a consequence, directly or indirectly, of the use and application of any of the contents of this book.

Lastly, this book is written under the right of the First Amendment to the Constitution of the United States. This book is written as an outside business activity from my investment advisory and securities business.

The ideas expressed are not meant to be taken as advice that you can act upon.

You should find an individual advisor that you trust to implement these ideas after determining if they are appropriate and suitable for your unique situation.

Introduction

"Rule #1: Never lose money. Rule #2: Never forget rule #1"

Warren Buffet

What you have in your hand is the 2016 Guide to Maximizing Your Retirement Income. The purpose of this book is to give you a simple way to look at your retirement and address what most seniors or pre-retirees are concerned about, which is having enough money to live the rest of their lives with the lifestyle that they want. The strategies and the products that clients can use are explained in this book.

I have over twenty-seven years of experience in the investment management business as of June 2016. During that period of time I've met with thousands of families and we literally have thousands of clients that have the same concern - will I run out of money in retirement?

The purpose of this guide is to not only give you simple strategies, but to boost your confidence and remove fear from your life when it comes to your retirement planning. This is about having cash flow in retirement to do what you want, when you want, and to be able to help your kids and grandkids or your loved ones if you choose to. But to be very clear, this book is about you first. This is about you maximizing your retirement income.

See, here's the problem that exists. Thousands and thousands of retirees and pre-retirees have gotten horrible advice. You're told to rely on your own devices. You watch CNBC and you get the hot stock of the day. You read Money Magazine or Kiplinger's, and you find out what are the five mutual funds that I should own this year. I would say that of all the abundance in the world of advice right now and the information that's available to us, you need to learn to sort out that information. None of us are suffering from the lack of information. What we really need is someone to help us cut through the clutter and find the information that's going to benefit us.

Quite frankly I think most people need an investment coach. Not the smartest person in the world. Not somebody running a hedge fund. Not somebody that's got twenty years with a big Wall Street investment firm. What people need is someone that's more of a coach. A coach to guide them, like my son's baseball coach does. The baseball coach is going to teach him based on his talents and his unique situation, how to best use those talents. How to best use what he has, quite frankly, to maximize his potential.

Well, that's what I want to do for you. I want you to be able to maximize the potential in your retirement income. I'm going to give you four basic sections in this book, and in each section there will be simple advice to help you maximize what you have regardless of where you're at right now.

We meet many people every single week at my firm, Johnson Brunetti. I do a weekly television & radio program where I share my experience with the public, with the sole purpose of providing value and knowledge to their lives. We also do many seminars in the area where I practice financial planning. So we get the opportunity to meet a lot of people and give a lot of second opinions, and sort of triage their financial situation if you will. There are some people who haven't saved enough for retirement, and then the coach needs to come in and help them either get back on track or change their expectations.

Other folks have saved more than enough, but they don't feel like it because they don't have anybody that's willing to lay out a plan for them and they don't have the confidence of knowing that they're going to be okay. Even though by all measurements they are going to be okay, they don't feel like it. This book is about giving you some tools and giving you some basic fundamentals to learn how to maximize your retirement income.

Chapter 1

Lower Your Taxes

There are all kinds of different taxes, but one of the clear keys to having more money available to spend is to pay less in taxes. Now I'm certainly not talking about cheating on your taxes. That is not the intent of this chapter. The intent of this chapter is to make sure that you are smart about where your investments are, where you're taking your income from, so that you don't pay more taxes than you absolutely have to. We want you to pay the minimum amount of taxes because that just simply means more money in your pocket.

We've had clients come into my firm and after doing a study of their tax return and where their investments are, sometimes we're able to save them a significant amount of taxes not only by reducing their income tax, but also by reducing taxes on their Social Security. One of the things I want you to understand is how the different types of income (earned, social security, interest) get taxed. So let's talk about some of the different types of taxes here.

There are about five different types of taxes we're going to talk about. Number one is taxes on your Social Security income. Number two is just traditional income tax. The third type is capital gains tax. The fourth type is taxes you pay when you take money out of your IRA or 401(k) or any other type of retirement account. The fifth type I want to talk about is taxes on annuities.

So let's dig in.

Social Security Income

First, let's talk about Social Security taxes. Many of you were told that when you become retired and get monthly Social Security checks that you wouldn't have to pay taxes on that money. As a matter of fact, that was the intent of Social Security; that the payments that you received in retirement would be tax-free. Well, that's not the case for a number of different reasons. The politicians have gone after Social Security and most of you have to include it in your taxable income when you retire. So if you're already retired you've learned this lesson. If you're not retired, you need to understand this.

Sometimes people don't pay any taxes on their Social Security income. Sometimes 50% of their Social Security income is exposed to taxes, meaning that if I get $20,000 a year in Social Security I have to pay taxes on $10,000 of it. For some folks 85% of their Social Security income is exposed to the taxman. Meaning again, for that $20,000 income from Social Security that I may be getting, $17,000 or 85% is exposed to taxes. What's the difference? The Social Security check can be the same. That $20,000 I'm receiving from Social Security can be exactly the same size check compared to my next door neighbor but depending on where my other income comes from, I could be exposed to higher taxes. So let's talk about some things that could trigger taxes on your Social Security. The two biggies are interest and dividends. There's also a third one which is tax-free income from municipal bonds.

Let's talk about interest that effects tax on Social Security for a minute. Many of the folks that we meet have money at the bank, and that money at the bank is in CDs, and it's in CDs because they feel that it is keeping their money safe. With CDs not being exposed to the stock market and being held at the bank it gives a sense of safety to these folks. Well, of course the CDs pay interest and most folks that have CDs at the bank don't take the interest. They leave the interest at the bank. They let the interest roll back or reinvest in the CD. However, at the end of the year they have to declare that as income on their tax return, and what happens is that additional interest income on your tax return goes into a formula that could trigger taxes on your Social Security.

Other types of interest income could be from mutual

funds. If you have a bond fund, there is interest paid on those bonds. You, like most of our clients, are reinvesting that interest. When you have a mutual fund, the fund pays a distribution at the end of the year, you just buy more shares. You don't even know what's happening sometimes. But yet that shows up on your tax return potentially triggering a tax again on your Social Security.

The other big item that impacts tax on Social Security is dividends. Now dividends are nice because they get taxed at a lower rate if they're qualified dividends. But dividends overall, whether they're qualified or not qualified, show up on your tax return. What happens is the IRS says okay, we're going to add up all your interest, all your dividends, all your tax-free municipal bond interest. We're going to add up all those numbers, we're going to take half of your Social Security and we're going to add all your other income, like pension income and earned income and so on. That is your "Provisional Income". We're going to add all that up and if you trigger a certain threshold, then you will be subject to Social Security taxes.

How Much of Your Social Security is Taxed?

Provisional Income	Percent of SS Benefits Taxed
Below $25,000 Single & Head of Household	**0%**
Below $32,000 Married Filing Jointly	**0%**
$25,000 to $34,000 Single & Head of Household	**50%**
$32,000 to $44,000 Married Filing Jointly	**50%**
Above $34,000 Single & Head of Household	**up to 85% of**
Above $44,000 Married Filing Jointly	**benefits + other income**

So the key here is not to pay taxes on interest and dividends that you're not using if at all possible. Let me give you an example. We talked earlier about that money at the bank. The money at the bank that's in a CD that's earning interest, you're not spending the interest. It's just rolling into the bank. You're reinvesting the interest into the CD. However, it's being added to your tax return. What if you had that same money in a fixed annuity? Fixed annuities are relatively safe. They're not FDIC insured, but I certainly think they're safe. You can have interest being paid out on that fixed annuity, but if you're not receiving the interest, if you're just letting it roll into the annuity, you don't have to declare that as taxable income. Now obviously you have to make a time commitment with the annuity like you do with a CD, but if you can defer those taxes you're saving taxes on your Social Security income. So that would be one idea.

Another idea is instead of mutual funds that pay big dividends at the end of the year, buy more tax efficient mutual funds. Especially if you're not pulling the dividends out and spending them. You can own exchange traded funds or tax efficient mutual funds that don't spin out those distributions every year and then, of course, you won't have to add that to your taxable income. The key on Social Security taxes is really paying attention to the other things that are going on in your tax return. This is what I help folks with all the time when they come in and visit with us at our firm. We look at their tax return and make sure before we start analyzing their investments that they are not paying more taxes than is absolutely necessary.

Income Taxes

Let's discuss traditional income taxes. Taxes we pay on our earned income or on our pension income. Also on any kind of deferred compensation payout we're getting from a former employer. If we're exercising stock options, all that falls into the area of income taxes. You need to be aware of where and when you can reduce your income taxes. Again, really what this comes down to is do you need all of the income that you're paying income taxes on? Sometimes there are ways to defer income. So we're not going to spend a lot of time here on income taxes, but just think of traditional income taxes differently than Social Security taxes which we talked about earlier.

Income taxes are any taxes on all of your income.

Earned income, unearned income, rental income, interest, dividends, distribution from retirement plans, etc... Now you might get confused. You might say here, well Joel, you just talked about how interest and dividends affect my Social Security taxes. Yes, I did. But that was your Social Security income that's being taxed. Now we're talking about potential double taxation if you will because it's on your other income. Any time you can reduce income while still having spendable money in retirement, you may be hitting a home run there. But again, that depends on your individual situation. So just be aware of your income taxes.

One trick that many clients have employed is that they'll take a certain amount of income in one year. Maybe they take $60,000 in one year and then they can manipulate their income so they take much lower income in the second year. So then maybe their living off of let's say $40,000 a year, but you're taking $60,000 one year and then only $20,000 the next. Well, that year that you're only taking twenty what's happening is that year you might not owe any income taxes at all. You might not pay any taxes on your Social Security either. So it's a way of staggering your income tax. For more details on that or how we've been able to successfully employ that with clients, feel free to call my office.

Capital Gains Taxes

Another type of tax is capital gains. These taxes are when we sell something and we have to pay a tax because we had a profit. Hopefully it's long-term capital gains. Short-term capital gains, when we sell something we've owned for less than a year, that is taxed as ordinary income. So if I buy a share of Exxon stock today and six months from now I sell it at a profit that is a short-term capital gain and that's going to get taxed just like regular income, at a higher tax bracket. But if I have long-term gains, an asset owned for more than one year, long-term gains for most of us are taxed at a much lower tax bracket.

There are a few areas where long-term gains come into

play for our clients. Number one could be a stock that I inherited. So let's say my mom or dad pass away and I inherit Apple stock, and let's pretend I inherited it ten years ago when it was worth a lot less money. Well when I inherit that stock, that's my ownership date for the purpose of establishing my tax cost. Now it's ten years later and I go to sell that Apple stock. Well, it's capital gains tax. It's long-term capital gains. So I get to add that on a different part of my return, and I'm only taxed at either 15% or 20% where on my regular income I could be taxed up to as much as 39.6% in 2016. So you can see how capital gains, long-term capital gains tax is much more favorable than ordinary income taxes. That's why it's very advantageous to own either individual stocks or exchange traded funds where there's not a lot of buying and selling going on in the exchange traded funds. Of course, with individual stocks, I get to control when the buying and selling is going on because then I don't have to pay taxes on money that I'm not using. The compound effect of owning assets over a long period of time without having to pay taxes is absolutely phenomenal.

I cannot express how exciting it is to own something like a piece of real estate or shares of stock, or maybe a piece of a business, that goes up in value, even if it's only increasing by 8-12% per year, just for the fact that you're not paying taxes on it. Then when you do sell it, you get to use the proceeds but you only have to pay the long-term capital gains tax rates on it which is very, very powerful. To wrap up capital gains tax, short-term means you've owned the asset for less than a year. Long-term simply means you've owned the asset for more than a year.

IRA, 401(k) & Other Retirement Plan Distributions

One of the other ways to reduce your taxes in retirement is to get control of your IRA and 401(k), and other retirement plan distributions. What do I mean by get control? I simply mean that at age 70½ the IRS forces us to begin taking distributions from any qualified retirement plans, which are IRAs, 401(k)s, 457 plans, 403(b) plans, and a few other less common plans.

The IRS forces us to take those distributions. There's only one exception to this, and that is if we have a 401(k) with a company that we're still working for. If we have a 401(k) with a company we're still working for then we don't have to take our required minimum distribution out of that particular 401(k).

Now this brings up an interesting possibility. What if you are working for a company, let's say AT&T. You're seventy-two years old. Still working there as an employee, and you have a 401(k) with them. You also have other IRAs and other retirement accounts and you'd just as soon not have to take money out of those other accounts because you don't need the income right now, but the IRS is forcing you to take money out of those other IRAs or retirement accounts because of course you're over 70½. You could actually take that money, roll it into the 401(k) at the company you're working at and now you don't have to take required minimum distributions on that AT&T 401(k) until again, you leave AT&T which we used in our example.

That's a little trick that you need to know about. But other than that what happens is that at age 70½ we're forced to take minimum required distributions.

Required minimum distributions for IRAs

Age of retiree	Distribution factor	Age of retiree	Distribution factor
70	27.4	93	9.6
71	26.5	94	9.1
72	25.6	95	8.6
73	24.7	96	8.1
74	23.8	97	7.6
75	22.9	98	7.1
76	22.0	99	6.7
77	21.2	100	6.3
78	20.3	101	5.9
79	19.5	102	5.5
80	18.7	103	5.2
81	17.9	104	4.9
82	17.1	105	4.5
83	16.3	106	4.2
84	15.5	107	3.9
85	14.8	108	3.7

86	14.1	109	3.4
87	13.4	110	3.1
88	12.7	111	2.9
89	12.0	112	2.6
90	11.4	113	2.4
91	10.8	114	2.1
92	10.2	115 or older	1.9

You can see on the table that at age 70½ you simply take the total amount of all your IRAs added up and you divide by 27.4 and you're going to come up with a number and that's the amount of money you have to take out of those retirement plans.

So what happens is you lose a certain amount of control at age 70½. Let's talk about the importance of control. Losing control is one of the worst things that you can do as a retiree. Remember what's going on psychologically as a retiree.

You've worked all your life. Especially in your fifties, you were probably in your peak earning years, maybe your sixties were your peak earning years, and then all of a sudden you stop working and you realize, I'm no longer earning money. I need to live off the money that I've saved. So you've already felt a little bit of a shift there, a fundamental shift, psychologically in losing a little bit of control, or a little bit of power.

The next thing that happens is the IRS comes along and says we're also going to have you lose control on your retirement accounts. The key here is to get out in front of these required minimum distributions. Quite frankly start thinking about this when you're sixty and sixty-five years old and saying well, if the IRS is going to take control of these retirement accounts and force me to start taking money out at age 70½, maybe I should come up with a plan when I'm sixty or sixty-five, or even sixty-eight to begin to reduce the potential force out of those accounts at age 70½. There are a couple of things you can do here. One is you could at age sixty-five for instance, freeze the growth of your IRA. Say every time my IRA goes up in value, I'm going to start taking a little bit of money. I'm going to maybe take those winnings if you will, off the table now and pull it out of that account so that I don't have a bigger problem when I'm 70½. You could convert money from a traditional IRA or retirement account over to a Roth. Now this means we have to pay some taxes today, but then that Roth IRA, as long as we follow some simple rules, that money is tax free for us forever. So we pay some taxes but then the money and the growth on that money is tax free forever. This is especially advantageous if you think taxes are going up. If you think taxes are going up, it definitely makes sense to consider converting some or possibly all of your retirement accounts. Now I said consider, I didn't tell you to do it. You really need to sit down with a financial professional and walk through the pros and cons of this ROTH conversion. But the key here is get control of your IRA and 401(k) distributions. Don't be foolish or complacent because that can trigger higher taxes.

The last thing I want to talk about is a little trick about how to lower your taxes in retirement. I would like to give you an example here. Let's say I have $1 million in non-retirement accounts or we could say I have $1 million in brokerage accounts. This could be broken up into different types of annuities, maybe different types of financial products or funds. I have $1 million saved up and it's not in IRAs. I decide out of that $1 million I want about a $60,000 a year income and I want that to last for the rest of my life. Six percent income is the goal.

Well, there's a number of ways I could do that. I could invest in different securities or different insurance products and just spin off $60,000 a year and spend it, but that would mean that my income is $60,000 a year and I have to pay taxes on that entire $60,000 a year. That may not be favorable. The other thing I could do is come up with a little trick called a laddered annuity plan, or a structured income plan. There are different names that advisors call it. That would look something like this.

I take that $1 million and divide it up into let's say four

sections. The first section would be probably about $270,000. I take that $270,000 and I buy a five-year immediate annuity. Which means that I'm giving that $270,000 to an insurance company and they're going to guarantee to pay me out all that money over the next five years. I'm going to get a little bit of interest, so I'll probably get about $60,000 a year for five years based on current rates.

Now what that means is when they pay me out that $60,000 for the first five years, remember $270,000 will be my original investment, and only $30,000 over that five-year period was interest. If I take the $30,000 of total interest I'm going to get over five years, divide that by five, that's about $6,000 of interest per year. That means I'm getting $60,000 of spendable money per year and I'm only paying income tax on $6,000 of it. So for the first five years of the retirement income that's coming off of that $1 million portfolio it's almost all tax free. In fact, it may all be tax free if I don't have too much other income as we discussed earlier.

Now what happens is at the end of the five-year period

I have spent down that $270,000, and I've got to tap into the next leg or the next rung of my annuity ladder that I've built. But the next rung of that annuity ladder is still going to be very tax-favored. Maybe for years six through ten, 70% of my income is completely tax free.

The idea you can see already is that I'm spending down these different pieces of money. So I've taken the first bucket and spent it down to zero. I'm now taking the second bucket from year's six to ten and spending it down to zero. The idea is buckets three and four are growing, and they should be growing faster than what I'm spending down and therefore, I'm keeping up. So if I pass away, my heirs potentially could get my original investment back. Especially if I layer life insurance into it.

I'm not trying to get into all the details of this laddered annuity strategy. I just want you to understand the power of that first five years, and maybe even the second five years, where much of your retirement income can be completely tax free. What that means is in the years when you are probably most active – traveling, visiting the kids and the grandkids, spending more money – you're paying less taxes. Now in the later years of your retirement, maybe in your late seventies and eighties, yes, you're going to have to pay taxes just as you would have if that would have all been ordinary income, all that $60,000, but maybe you don't care as much then. It's about getting more money in your pocket in the early years of your retirement.

These different ways to lower taxes again are ideas that may be helpful to you. The purpose of this chapter is to get you thinking about the different types of taxes and how they may apply to you. If you get in front of a professional, a good trustworthy professional in your area that not only understands investments but also taxes, they can help structure the proper plan for you. I would advise you to seek out an investment advisor that completely understands taxes. Not a tax person that thinks they understand investments, because those are very few and far between. If you get in front of an investment advisor that really understands taxes they can improve your cash flow and do some very, very interesting things so that you don't pay more taxes than you have to, and the idea is that you have more spendable income. The goal is more after-tax income for those critical retirement years.

Annuities

Annuities can be set up to have a very, very favorable tax treatment which will increase your spendable income, meaning your after-tax income. It's important to think about and plan for the early years of your retirement when you are able to do many things. Then plan for the later years of life when maybe you don't have the energy or the physical ability to do the things you used to be able to do. It's about maximizing your spendable income when you need it the most and then maybe you pay a little bit more in taxes in the later years of your life when you may not be as physically active to spend the extra money anyway. It's just some smart tax planning here.

Chapter 2

Invest with a Bias towards Income-Producing Securities & Products

The next key to maximizing retirement income that we're going to talk about is investing with a bias towards income-producing securities and products.

What are income-producing securities and products? These are investments that are designed to produce income but you could also have some growth in the particular investment. Let's just talk about the real basic difference between a growth type investment and an income type investment. A growth type investment is typically an investment that I'm going to buy and let's say it is shares in the technology company

LinkedIn. It's an investment that doesn't pay an income so I don't get a dividend from it. I just buy the shares, hope the shares are going to go up in value and I don't want any current income while I hold the shares. That is an example of a growth investment.

An example of a growth and income, or income-producing investment could be if I own for instance stock in a company that paid a big dividend. A company like AT&T pays a very, very nice dividend and usually the dividend on AT&T is somewhere around 4-5%. So I can buy the shares, hope the shares go up, but while I'm holding the shares I'm continuing to get dividends on the shares. So I'm getting paid to hold the stock if you will. That's an example of a growth and income investment.

What we want to do if we're interested in maximizing retirement income is to have a goal towards more income or have a bias towards more income-producing assets. Now these could be annuities. These could be real estate investment trusts which are referred to as

REITs. These could be high yielding bonds. These could be stocks that pay dividends. These could be things like oil and gas master-limited partnerships that pay very high dividends. We're going to go through some of these different things. Please understand that I'm not recommending one of these or all of these to you in your individual situation. It is critical that you get with somebody that's a good financial advisor who you can trust that can help show you the pros and the cons, the good and the bad, towards these different investments so that you can sift through and filter out the things that are not right for you.

Dividend-Paying Stocks

Stocks that pay dividends are traditionally more mature companies. I'm just going to rattle off some names here, these are all stocks that pay nice dividends. Some of them I own. Chevron. Exxon. IBM. Apple Computer. Pfizer. Merck. These are all companies where if I own their stock, yes, I'm hoping the shares go up over time but I'm getting paid to hold the stock.

Let's take Chevron stock for instance. Say I've owned Chevron stock for a number of years, and when I bought it, it was paying about a 3% dividend. If I put $100,000 into it for example, I'm getting paid $3,000 per year to own the stock. Now let's think about the safety of that investment for a minute. If I'm getting paid $3,000 a year to own the stock and I put in $100,000, that's obviously a 3% yield. If I put that $100,000 in the bank at the same time I had bought the Chevron stock, I would not be receiving a 3% yield. I'd probably only be getting 1% yield. Also, if I put that money in the bank I wouldn't get any growth on my money. All I'm guaranteed is to get my money back. With Chevron stock, I don't have a guarantee, but in my opinion Chevron is not going to go out of business as long as I am alive. Therefore, I think that not only is my investment somewhat secure, even though I know the price of the shares will fluctuate, I'm getting paid 3% dividend and over time Chevron has increased its dividends. So my yield on my original investment is going to go up. That's an example of a high dividend paying stock.

Now you have to understand that in the income-producing investment category, dividend-paying stocks are one of the more risky things because they are going to go up and down in value. It's an important part of the whole picture here when we're considering income-producing securities.

Equity Income Type Mutual Funds

The second category would be equity income type mutual funds. So if I don't want to get into picking stocks I can pick individual mutual funds. In a mutual fund, the mutual fund itself owns a group or a bundle of stocks. Let's take a fund called Fidelity Equity Income Fund. Well, Fidelity Equity Income Fund might own 100 or 200 different stocks or different companies within that fund. I buy one fund but there's a money manager at Fidelity that goes through and chooses the stocks that he thinks are the best ones to own.

Now all those stocks or most of those stocks are going

to pay a dividend. So I could have them pay me out the dividends that the stocks inside that fund are paying and that dividend yield is 2-3%. In addition to the dividend, the share price of the mutual fund should go up if they're picking good companies inside the mutual fund because of course those company shares underlying the mutual fund should also go up in value. So again, I'm getting growth and income from this investment.

As you realized from these first two categories - dividend-paying stocks and equity income type mutual funds - I'm only going to get somewhere around a 3% yield unless I buy super high yielding dividend-paying stocks. Let's just say I buy the normal ones that are going to pay me about a 3% dividend. That may not be enough income for you but you're going to get price appreciation. So maybe you don't have your whole portfolio in equity income funds or dividend-paying stocks but you have a portion of it invested this way. Because the equity income mutual fund and the dividend-paying stocks over time should appreciate in value so you also have some inflation protection.

High Yield Bonds

We like high yield bonds at our firm Johnson Brunetti for a portion of someone's portfolio. An example of a high yield bond could be a bond by a company like Verizon which most of us are familiar with where they're not as safe necessarily as General Electric or Wal-Mart, but I still think they're a pretty darned good company and I might be able to buy a Verizon bond that pays me a 5-6% interest rate. That would be a very nice interest rate. You'll notice the interest rate is higher than the dividend-paying stocks and that's mostly because it's a bond. From a legal standpoint a bond from a company is safer than a stock from the same company.

We like bond funds, high yield bond funds and high yield exchange traded funds in our portfolios for our clients. In fact, I've got one custom portfolio I designed for our clients and it pays about a 5½% yield. It's got a lot of high yield bond funds in it, and high yield exchange traded funds, some stocks, but mostly high yield bond funds and high yield exchange traded funds. It pays a very nice income that folks can spend right now if they want to, and although the share price will go up and down, it's fairly stable over time. Historically speaking, if I look back at the writing of this book over the last ten years, a good basket of high yield bond funds or a mutual fund or an exchange traded fund, the historical total rate of return on that is somewhere around 6 to 7% without as much volatility as the stock market. So we favor high yield bond funds at our firm, but again do a complete and full investigation before you decide whether that is right for you or be sure to find a competent financial advisor.

Real Estate Trusts

Another income-producing security that you could own is a real estate trust and what we like about real estate trusts is that the underlying real estate provides an inflation edge. Over time real estate has been one of the best performing assets to own when it comes to inflation and in addition to that, commercial real estate whether it's apartment buildings, office buildings, warehouses or retail facilities like Wal-Marts or CVS's or Home Depots – they spin off rental income.

There are two types of real estate trusts. There is a non-traded real estate trust and there is a traded real estate trust. A traded real estate trust trades just like a stock. They tend to pay lower dividends and the share price bounces up and down every single day in the stock market. A non-traded real estate trust does not trade like a stock. In fact, you give up liquidity when you buy a non-traded real estate trust. For example, I personally owned a non-traded real estate trust and it was all healthcare properties all around the U.S. I enjoyed a 6.6% dividend from that. So I put $50,000 into it, I received a 6.6% dividend every month that I could have spent if I wanted to. Over time the value of that real estate went up, so it also acted as an inflation hedge. This can be very attractive for someone who's getting ready to retire or is in retirement. Because remember, the key in retirement is when you're taking income off a portfolio, you don't want to be overly exposed to stock market risk. If the market goes way down and you continue to pull income off a portfolio it's going to either erode the portfolio down to zero over time, or you're going to have to cut your income back because now you have to sell more shares to produce that income. I'm in a much better position with something where the share price is more stable and I can spend the dividends and hopefully get appreciation on the share price. I don't have to sell when the market is low. So we use this non-traded real estate trust when suitable for our clients - and again folks, don't go out and buy these on your own. You need to have a financial advisor that you trust that can show you the pros and cons. When suitable for clients, they've been very, very effective for us overall. Again, they can pay 5-6% dividend yield and over time I have the potential for the share price going up.

I'll give you one example. There's a company out there

called Healthcare Trust of America. It trades on the New York Stock Exchange under the symbol HTA. Well, HTA, we sold to our clients into their portfolios and when they bought HTA back when it was a non-traded real estate trust it was trading at $10 per share. They collected a 7% dividend for a period of about two to three years while they held their shares. So they were getting paid 7% just to hold their shares. They could spend that money or reinvest it. Then that non-traded real estate trust listed on the New York Stock Exchange and became a traded one, and as of the writing of this book, which is near the end of 2015, our clients paid $10, they got a 7% dividend, the stock listed on the New York Stock Exchange, today they can sell at $12 (adjusted for splits) per share if they want to, which is an additional 20% profit or they can hold those shares and continue to collect the dividend. So real estate trusts are also an excellent tool when suitable as far as producing income in retirement. Be aware these are not safe or guaranteed investments, they do have some risk.

*Past performance does not guarantee future results.

Annuities

The last tool with a bias towards an income-producing account is an annuity, and there are four different types of annuities, I'm going to go through these very, very briefly then I'm going to hone in on one particular annuity which is an annuity designed for income where you don't have to give up control of your principal.

Annuity number one is just simply a fixed annuity. If you understand the CD you understand the fixed annuity. I can go out and buy a five-year fixed annuity which means I deposit my money with the insurance company and I leave it alone for five years. I can collect let's say a 3% interest rate for five years, and then at the end of that five years I can take my money and I can do whatever I want with it. So I made a time commitment for five years. I get 3% for five years. That's a lot like a five-year CD. It's not issued by a bank, and it's not FDIC insured, but that is a fixed annuity. Very, very simple. Safety with no fees.

The second type of annuity is a variable annuity. In a variable annuity I'm still buying an account from an insurance company but inside that annuity are all kinds of mutual fund choices. I still have stock market risks in a variable annuity on my principal, however in a variable annuity for an extra fee inside the account I can get a minimum income guarantee. Right now there's another company out there, where as a 65-year-old I could give them $500,000 and we'd put it in a variable annuity and they will guarantee me 5% income from that for as long as I live. I get to pick the mutual funds or the investments inside that annuity.

But if my picks are really bad and the account goes to zero, as long as I don't take out more than the 5% per year, the insurance company is still going to pay me the 5% for as long as I live. That's called a variable annuity with an income rider or an income guarantee on it. That can be pretty attractive if I want the upside of the market. Again, the variable annuity gives me some upside of the market, but I also have the downside of the market. However, I have a minimum guarantee on my income if I choose to structure it that way.

The third type of annuity is an immediate annuity, and that just simply means I take my money and I give it to the insurance company. So I've given up control of my money. If I give the same $500,000 to the insurance company as a 65-year-old they might guarantee me 6½% on that money for as long as I live. I've given up access to my principal, I actually don't own the $500,000 anymore. They're giving me 6½% for as long as I live but if I die too soon, I could die before I get the $500,000 out. If I live really long, then I've beaten the insurance company at their own game. These first three annuities aren't as popular as the next one I'm going to tell you about. The next one I'm going to tell you about we use a lot in my financial services practice for our clients and this is called the index annuity, and in particular the index annuity with a guaranteed minimum income rider on it. Let's talk about the index annuity. The index annuity, again I can take that $500,000 and put it in an account. My principal is guaranteed by the insurance company.

If the stock market index drops, I lose no money. If the index goes up, I can earn interest based on that index. Now I'm not going to go up or I'm not going to get as much interest as I would have gotten in the good years if my money was in the stock market. I am giving up some upside potential in return for them taking away the downside risk.

Now again, there are a lot more details than this but I'm trying to keep the conversation simple here. The bottom line is that I've got principal protection and over time I can get a reasonable rate of return on the index annuity that should be higher than a CD or a fixed annuity if we look back over history. Now I can add to the index annuity what we call an income rider, which can be very powerful. There's one company out there right now where I can put in let's say that $500,000 and they'll guarantee me a 7% increase in my income account value for every year that I leave the account alone. If I leave the account alone for ten years the <u>income value</u> on that $500,000 will become almost $1 million. I can't just take out that $1 million in one lump sum but what I can do is I can take income off of that, a percentage of income off of that $1 million account value. That $1 million could pay me out as much as 5%, 5½%, 6% depending on my age. So I've invested an original amount of maybe $500,000. I've waited for ten years. And then maybe I can get $60,000 a year guaranteed for as long as I live.

Now with these annuities, there's a lot of details I'm not going into here. So please understand, I'm not recommending the annuity. This becomes a one-on-one conversation that needs to happen with a good financial advisor for you, but it's worth investigating. (By the way I have never heard of anyone at a big stock brokerage firm recommend these products. I will let you figure out why.)

All of these things that I've mentioned – the dividend-paying stocks, the equity income type mutual funds, the high yield bonds and high yield bond funds, the real estate trusts and the annuities will produce a nice income for you that may be much higher than some of the things you're using now and they're somewhat removed from stock market volatility, depending on which category that you tend to use.

In this chapter we have talked about investing with a bias towards income-producing security and products. The reason this is so important is because so many folks that we visit with that come in for an appointment at my firm have been trying to do everything with mutual funds. They've been trying to create a secure retirement with mutual funds. They've got a basket of mutual funds whether it's in their 401(k) or elsewhere and they're moving towards retirement within five years or maybe they're in retirement and they're just riding this rollercoaster of the stock market. Up one year, down the next, up for a few years and then the big down. It's causing all kinds of problems in their lives emotionally and quite frankly, they're losing sleep at night.

Our answer to that is to have a bias towards income-producing investments. As a retiree, let's say you're sixty-five years old, maybe you ought to have 65% to 75% of your money in income-producing assets and maybe 25% of your money is actually in pure stock market type things for growth. That way, you don't have to touch the stock market piece. When the times are bad you can leave the pure stock piece alone to recover because your income needs are being met from those income-producing products that we talked about. Which are the annuities, the real estate trusts, the high yield bond funds, the equity income funds, and so on. This is a different approach that we have found to be much more effective. Yes, it's simple but it's much more effective in my opinion than what we see some folks going through. Many of you are experiencing a lot of insecurity and a lot of sleepless nights because you're not sure how the market is going to perform and you are worried about losing money in retirement.

Chapter 3

Protect Against Inflation

There are two main reasons why inflation is so, so critical to plan for. The first reason is that we're living longer, the second reason is because of the fiscal policy of the United States. Because we're borrowing more and more money, there's a high probability that inflation at some point in our lifetime could be worse than what we've experienced in the decade of the '90s and the decade of the 2000s. But the main thing I want to focus on here for this particular chapter is the longevity risk.

Statistics tell us that if I'm sitting down with a couple that are both age sixty-five there is a high possibility that one of them (if not both of them) will live into their nineties. If you think back twenty years ago and somebody would die at sixty-five we would say, oh they lived a good life. Now if somebody dies at sixty-five we say, oh my goodness they died so young. Just think about how our mentality has changed towards longevity.

Well, add to that the fact that medicine is getting better, doctors are able to keep us alive longer, we're learning, we're much better educated now about nutrition and fitness and so on. Most of the folks that we see that are retired are living very, very vital meaningful lives. They are volunteering in their communities and waking up in the morning with vigor for life. Those folks are going to live for a much longer time, so it is key that we factor in inflation into their retirement income plan. This is important because of this longevity risk and also because of our government's fiscal policy.

I think at a minimum you should count on at least 3% inflation per year. We have folks that come in to us and we engage in a conversation with them about this.

Some of them are concerned with much higher inflation rates and so we'll factor that into their income plan. But count on at least 3% inflation. In very simple terms what that means is that if it costs me $5,000 a month to live this year, the next year I'd better have $5,150 a month, and the following year I'd have to have $5,314.50 a month, and so on. I need to be able to give myself 3% raises every single year. Which is why just taking all our money and putting it in the bank and collecting interest usually is not a good solution for most of us. It's in our best interest to factor in at least 3% inflation.

Historically speaking, if we go back and we take the year 2014 and go back over a thirty-year period, inflation has been at around 3%. If you're concerned about government policies, about U.S. borrowing, the national debt, our constant budget deficits, and all the promises that we've made as far as Medicare and Social Security then you might want to factor in a 4% or 5% long-term inflation rate to your retirement plan. If you go online and play with some of those income calculators or those retirement calculators that are available on Vanguard and Fidelity and T. Rowe Price and so on and you start factoring in 5% inflation, you'll find out very quickly you'd better be getting very, very good rates of return on your money to keep up with that inflation. So inflation is critical. When we plan for our clients, we plan for a minimum of at least 3%.

Let's talk about some investments that protect us against inflation. We've already mentioned some of these things, but I want to touch on them one more time. So first of all, real estate has been a tremendous hedge against inflation. That's primarily because real estate reflects replacement costs of the assets. For example, the seven story office building where our firm resides was built about twenty or twenty five years ago. To build the exact same building today would cost much more than it did twenty or twenty five years ago. This is because the steel, the sheetrock, the concrete, all the electrical, the pipes, all of those materials cost much more today. So therefore, the building that I'm sitting in is worth much more than it was twenty-five years ago. Why? Because the replacement cost is higher.

If I owned this building, I've been collecting rent all those years and there's been two things that have happened over time. One is I've been able to raise the rent because again as inflation kicks in, renters have to pay more money, and if I'm a landlord collecting that rent my income goes up along with inflation. Secondly, the value of the building that I own, the value of the asset goes up because the replacement cost is more. So I'm not only getting raises on my cash flow, but I'm also able to sell the building at a future date for much more than I paid for it.

Now this doesn't always work in the short-term. Some of you are thinking right now about what's happening in the housing market in the U.S. and the commercial real estate market in the U.S. since 2007. I understand that, but that is a relatively short-term period of time. If you're planning for retirement, you're planning on ten, twenty, thirty years or more of retirement then I think real estate is a good inflation hedge to own.

Another good inflation hedge to own is stocks. The problem with stocks is that we have to watch them go up and down every day. But stocks as an asset class, what you really have there is you have ownership in great companies. If I'm not trying to beat the market and just buy real hot stocks and I'm buying really good companies that I think are going to be around for a long time then I should certainly keep up with inflation as far as value goes. Let's just think about a few here together, Coca Cola, General Electric, United Technologies, AT&T, Wal-Mart, Kimberly Clark and Merck, which is the big pharmaceutical company. Those types of companies, good healthy companies that have a lot of cash flow, might be around for a long time. The values of those businesses should go up over time, or at least if I have a basket of 100 stocks, most of the business values will go up over time. In addition, as mentioned earlier, I can collect some dividends. So stocks can be a very good inflation hedge.

Now again, the problem with stocks is people don't want to see them go up and down. You get a statement in the mail and when your account is down 10-20% from just three months earlier that's very unsettling, and you begin to wonder if you'll ever recover. So stocks are not appropriate for everybody, and they're certainly not appropriate for too much of your portfolio in retirement. But I'm mentioning them here as an inflation hedge.

So we talked about real estate. We've talked about stocks. Now in addition to that, a pretty good hedge against inflation is an annuity that will give us increases in income over time. Right now there's a big company that we use. I own two annuities from that particular company. I won't mention the name.
When I begin to take income off of my annuity, they'll take the income value of the annuity and if I'm sixty-five, they'll start me out at 5% of whatever the value is. So let's say the value is $500,000 and I'm sixty-five.

They're going to start paying me $25,000 a year. That

$25,000 a year is guaranteed for the rest of my life, no matter how the underlying account does. In addition to that, every year that the stock market indexes go up, I will get a raise. So every few years in that annuity I should get a raise that will in a sense give me kind of a cost of living allowance raise like a pension does. This is very, very attractive. So annuities can be a decent inflation hedge if they're the right kind. Again, not all annuities work like this, so they have to be the right kind.

Other assets that can protect against inflation would be direct ownership of things like oil or natural gas. You could have some precious metals or an exchange traded fund or a mutual fund that invests in precious metals. This can become very risky, so you have to be very careful in that area.

One particular investment that we also use, however, is something called master limited partnerships. This can be a very good inflation hedge and it can also pay you very nice incomes. For example, there is a company called Kinder Morgan they own pipelines all across the United States. They're the underground pipelines where natural gas and oil are piped through and sometimes they're over ground. What Kinder Morgan does is they basically own the pipe and then if Shell Oil wants to ship oil or natural gas from the port of Houston up into Denver for instance, they run it through Kinder Morgan's pipelines, and Kinder Morgan collects a toll, if you will, on that oil and gas. Think of Kinder Morgan as charging rent to Shell Oil to occupy their pipeline.

Well, because I'm getting rent off the pipeline, I'm getting an income, but also remember the replacement cost of the pipeline, just like real estate, is going up in value. So that can act over time as an inflation hedge. This gives you another option to invest in something that will protect against inflation.

The last inflation hedge I want to mention is the inflation-protected bonds put out by the U.S. government. We can buy what is called I Bonds from the U.S. government, or we can actually go out and buy a fund that invests in I Bonds. Now I'll be the first one to admit that I'm not a real expert in this area. The reason I'm not a big expert in this area is because quite frankly, the I Bonds have been a disappointment, in my opinion, since they've come out. A lot of people that own them are disappointed. A part of the reason is inflation hasn't been very present over the last few years, at least the inflation that the I Bonds measure. These are something to be considered, especially if you like the safety and guarantee of the U.S. government. An inflation-protected bond can pay you interest, and that interest can be pegged at the rate of inflation, so that may be an attractive alternative.

In this chapter we've discussed different things to invest in to protect against inflation. These are all strategies to maximizing your retirement income.

Chapter 4

Get a Retirement Income Plan

Establishing a retirement income plan may be the most important thing that I talk about in this book. I think every person concerned about their retirement income that is either in retirement or planning for retirement, should have a retirement income plan. I'm going to give you the components of a retirement income plan and talk about why this is important.

Many times whether you have a lot of money or just a little bit of money, we get caught up in the here and now. We look at what interest rates are down at the bank. We look at the interest rates we can earn if we buy a fixed annuity. We look at what kinds of rates of return are happening in the stock market, and we turn on the news and we hear the market was up and the market was down, and all of that thinking is very, very short-term. A retirement income plan gives you the confidence or it gives you at least the truth about where you stand in retirement based on certain assumptions. This is why I believe everyone should have their own unique retirement income plan.

What is a retirement income plan? It's simply a snapshot of where you are today, what you can earn on your money, and how long your money will last depending on how you live. It's a plan for income during your retirement years. Whether you're already retired, approaching retirement or planning for retirement, I think you need a retirement income plan. My recommendation is to have a professional Certified Financial Planner™ or at least a firm that has Certified Financial Planners™, put together a retirement income plan for you. You need somebody that is an expert in working with retirees and pre-retirees. You need an experienced professional that is going to know the hurdles that you will face when you get into retirement.

You could try to do this yourself, but many people don't have the wisdom or experience that the retirement specialist has. So again, in my opinion, get a retirement income plan, prepared by a professional retirement specialist.

Let's talk about the different steps necessary in developing a good retirement income plan. What I simply mean by the retirement income plan is, you have a piece of paper in your hand that says based on your situation how long your money should last given certain assumptions.

Here are the steps.

A. First of all, determine how much income you want. Pretend you're either retired today, and maybe you are, but if you're still working, pretend you're retired today. How much do you want coming into the house every single month in cash? That is net, after taxes. This is really important. Don't complicate it. Don't think about inflation right now. Don't think about rates of return on investments. Just write down the amount of money you want coming into the house every single month net after taxes. Let's say your number is $5,000, then write down $5,000.

B. Factor in some contingencies. So you need to create a side fund, if you will, to meet the big contingencies. These might be things like additional healthcare costs that aren't covered by your Medicare supplement or your health insurance. It might be emergencies. It might be things like helping the kids. It might be home maintenance costs. But we want to create a separate side fund so that you've got two groups of money. One group is your emergency money, your side fund, your liquidity money for all the other things, but the other group is your core nest egg. The core nest egg is your investment money. The job of the core nest egg, is to produce income for you for as long as you live. So factor in some contingencies and build up a side fund.

This is your emergency money. I would say somewhere around six to twelve months of income should be set aside and not counted in this retirement equation. When I say determine where you are now, add up all your savings and investments, but set aside some money that's not in that equation, because it's important you have extra money to fix the furnace, to fix the car, to buy a new car, to help out the kids or the grandkids. This includes those things that come up in life that you don't want to tap into your main investment accounts for. You want to have money set aside for that.

We're told statistically that a retired couple now might spend up to $250,000 during retirement on various healthcare things that aren't covered by insurance. Another big contingency is of course, long-term care or nursing home care, whether we need it in a nursing home or in our homes. I would certainly encourage you to explore buying insurance to cover that need. There are different types of long-term care insurance. There's the old fashioned kind where you pay a premium for the rest of your life, and there's a new kind that's kind of a hybrid where if you never use the long-term care benefit, you still get all your money back, or your beneficiaries get all your money back. But either one, you should explore shelving that risk or let's say shifting that risk to an insurance company.

C. The next thing you want to do is factor inflation into the mix. As we talked about earlier, I would factor in at least 3% inflation which means if you need $5,000 today then each year you need to give yourself a 3% compound raise. You're going to see where that adds up pretty quickly. So if you retire today and inflation is 3%, then in about twenty years you're going to need twice as much income as you do today.

D. Now what you want to do next after we have those first three steps; you want to determine where you're at now. How much do you have in existing savings and investments, in 401(k)s, in IRAs, in brokerage accounts?

Also part of determining where you are now is if you're still working; how much are you adding to your accounts? Are you adding $10,000, $15,000 or $20,000 per year like you could in 401(k)s or other types of retirement plans? What you want to do next is assume a certain rate of return. I think a 6% long-term rate of return is fairly safe to assume if your money is invested properly. Let me talk a little bit about this 6% rate of return.

Historically the market, going way way back into the '20s has returned somewhere around, depending on what you measure and if you count dividends or not, 8-9%. We know when we're taking income off of a portfolio we can't be

100% sure of the market because we run the risk of running our money down to zero in the bad times. So we can't completely be in the market at that 8-9%. We need to get better than let's say government bond rates, so that's where I'm coming up with this 6%. I think a well constructed portfolio, especially if you're working with a good financial planner and investment advisor should average 6% or more with "low" volatility. I think you should hold their feet to the fire and make sure that advisor over a three-to-five year period is delivering somewhere around a 6-7% rate of return so you are able to sleep at night. Now maybe they're doing better, but they should at least be getting that 6-7% rate of return. In my opinion that's doable. Not guaranteed, but possible.

Let's recap the steps we've gone through so far.

A. Determining how much income you want per month.

B. Factor in contingencies such as healthcare costs and emergencies.
C. Factor inflation into the mix as well and remember I said to use at least 3%.
D. Determining where you are now with existing savings and investments, how much you might be adding if you are still saving money and assuming about a 6% rate of return.

The results will show you how long your money should last. If you go and try to do this yourself, you would go online and find a good retirement income calculator. Use some of the websites from insurance companies and mutual fund companies. I would highly suggest however, that you do this with a professional. This will give you a reasonable expectation based on where you are now, how much income you want and how long you can expect your money to last. The last most important component here is to invest accordingly. Be cautious. Don't take too much risk. So many retirees we see coming into our office have been talked into taking too much risk, or think they have to take a lot of risk. What we've really found as we begin to investigate retiree's individual circumstances is that they have been good savers, and they don't need to take too much risk. Many times at least one spouse if not both spouses are very comfortable in knowing that they don't have to take too much risk.

Author Notes

In conclusion, the book you have in your hand presents some basic concepts for maximizing your retirement income. This book is not meant to be the end all and be all, and discuss every single detail of different investments you can have, different calculations you can do, and certainly is not a writing on economic policy. It's just a means to keep things simple and hopefully shift your thinking as a retiree or as somebody who is planning towards retirement so that you can have more confidence in what you're doing and to give you some direction whether you use a financial advisor or not. I want you to understand that the proper use of these products and investments are to increase cash flow in your retirement. When you find that retirement coach, that financial advisor that's the right person and you feel understands and cares about you, and has your best interest at heart; when you find that right person, you will be able to enjoy a wonderful and happy retirement.

How to Find the Right Financial Advisor

Here are nine important points you should keep in mind when you try to find the correct financial advisor. It is important that there is "chemistry" between you, that there is a good fit and a sharing of values. There also should be a feeling that the person understands you.

1. Independent

It is very important that the financial advisor you choose be independent, someone who is not an employee of a large firm. There are many firms at which brokers and advisors can work. I started in the business 27 years ago as an employee of a big brokerage firm, and we employees were told what products and funds to recommend. We were told that what we had to sell was perfect for everyone. When our sales manager had certain stocks that he would decide we should push in a certain month, guess what? Those stocks were what most people ended up owning.

I soon came to realize that this was the wrong approach, but unfortunately it still goes on today. Let's take, for example, a very large Wall Street brokerage firm. First of all, if you work for such a firm, the people you work with are employees of that firm, so their primary responsibility is to that firm, not to you. Their job is to increase shareholder value for that particular firm. You're just a customer.

However, if you work with an independent financial advisor, then you are the only person to whom that advisor answers. An ethical independent financial advisor does not have an agenda or a list of stocks to push. It is very important that you find an independent financial advisor.

2. Chemistry

The second important consideration is "chemistry." It's very important that you feel the person you're talking to understands you. If you are a husband and wife, make sure the person talks to both of you and also listens to both of you. If for one moment you feel that a broker is dismissing you or your feelings or is insulting or is coming across as arrogant, this is the wrong person to work with. You need to choose an advisor who understands you, who listens to you, and who will put together a financial plan that fits your needs and goals.

3. Empathy

Does the advisor understand you and feel like you do when it comes to your important issues? You may have a special-needs child who requires special planning. You may come from a very poor family, one that lived through the depression, and you're worried about running out of money. Can that advisor relate? It's critical that the advisor listen and feel empathy for your particular fears. Another clue that you're working with the wrong advisor is he or she does not understand or does not listen.

4. Adequate Staffing

Staffing is a critical issue: it's where the rubber meets the road in today's financial world. Make sure the advisor you work with has plenty of service staff, and do so by simply asking. I know some firms where a broker handles hundreds of accounts without a full-time assistant or maybe sharing one with another broker. This isn't going to work very well. Two things can happen. Number one, the service level drops; number two, the broker or advisor has to constantly answer every phone call, every service inquiry. If I am talking to my advisor, I want one who is thinking about my investments, one who deals one-on-one with clients, not one bogged down by service inquiries and other issues that could be handled by a service assistant or a customer service representative.

Our firm has six advisors and a team of 15 full-time and 2 part-time people. Each advisor has four backup people, and that's a pretty good ratio. I think you want at least a two-to-one ratio, two assistants per advisor in the firm. So a firm with two advisors should have at least four staff people backing them up. If you get lower than this in today's economy, when investment firms and insurance companies push more and more paperwork out to the financial firm than they used to do for their advisors, it is going to be very hard for that broker to handle your account.

5. Community Recognition

The broker or advisor you choose should have a recognized name in the community. Let's think about a company like Disney. In Orlando, if somebody even writes the word *Disney* on a sign, Disney comes after them to take that word down. Disney makes sure that if it has the legal right to force the issue, it will do it simply because it wants to protect its reputation, a reputation second to none.

Other companies such as McDonalds and Coca Cola that have a very high level of service and brand recognition will do almost anything to protect that brand. They will decide not to take certain customers because they worry that those customers might be the complaining type, and the companies want to protect their reputation and their brand.

The same goes for financial advisors. Financial advisors who have a recognized name in a community will be very careful to bend over backward to do the right thing because they have spent years building their strong reputations and don't want to do anything to tarnish them. Choose an advisor who has a well-recognized name in the community.

6. Author = Authority

It is important that your advisor be an author. Has yours written articles? Has yours authored books? Does he have any kind of ownership of publications out there, including a website? Is the website part of a big firm like Merrill Lynch or Ameriprise, or is it independent ?

Independent advisors will tend to have their own websites, not websites that are linked to big brokerage houses. It's helpful to know that your advisor has the expertise and the independence to write about subjects that are relevant to you.

7. Media Presence

This goes along with number six - find an advisor who has a media presence, someone the media trusts for knowledge and advice. TV and radio stations typically have certain people they go to in the community who are able to speak on a number of different subjects. Has your advisor been on TV or the radio in the role of a local expert? This can be a good indication of a good reputation.

8. A Good Business Person

Does your advisor know how to run a business? This goes back to the difference between an independent advisor and one who is just an employee of the firm. How somebody can handle millions of dollars of other people's money and have no clue how to run a business is beyond me. It's also beyond me that somebody would choose to work with an advisor who has no employees, who has no banking relationship or even a business checkbook, and who does not spend his or her own money on marketing and reputation. This is inconceivable to me.

Find an advisor who is independent and also understands the ins and outs of running a business, including hiring and firing employees, supervising customer service staff, and delegating issues as they come up instead of doing absolutely everything themselves.

9. Giving to the Community

Last but not least, find an advisor who gives to his or her community. Someone willing to put money into the community organically, not just for the sake of publicity such as sponsoring charity auctions so that an advisor can be seen with a prominent group. I'm talking about someone who is genuinely interested in supporting their community and will display a presence to those in need.

Keep these nine considerations in mind when you are in the process of choosing a financial advisor. Also try to make an individual list of your own values to expand upon the ones I have offered above. After all, this is about you and no one can protect you better then yourself. Start with my list and begin to narrow down the advisors in your community; it is very possible that in an area like Connecticut, my state which has thousands of licensed financial advisors, you may come up with only 20 to choose from. But then you can begin to interview them, talking and listening, and end up with the one who is the best fit for you.

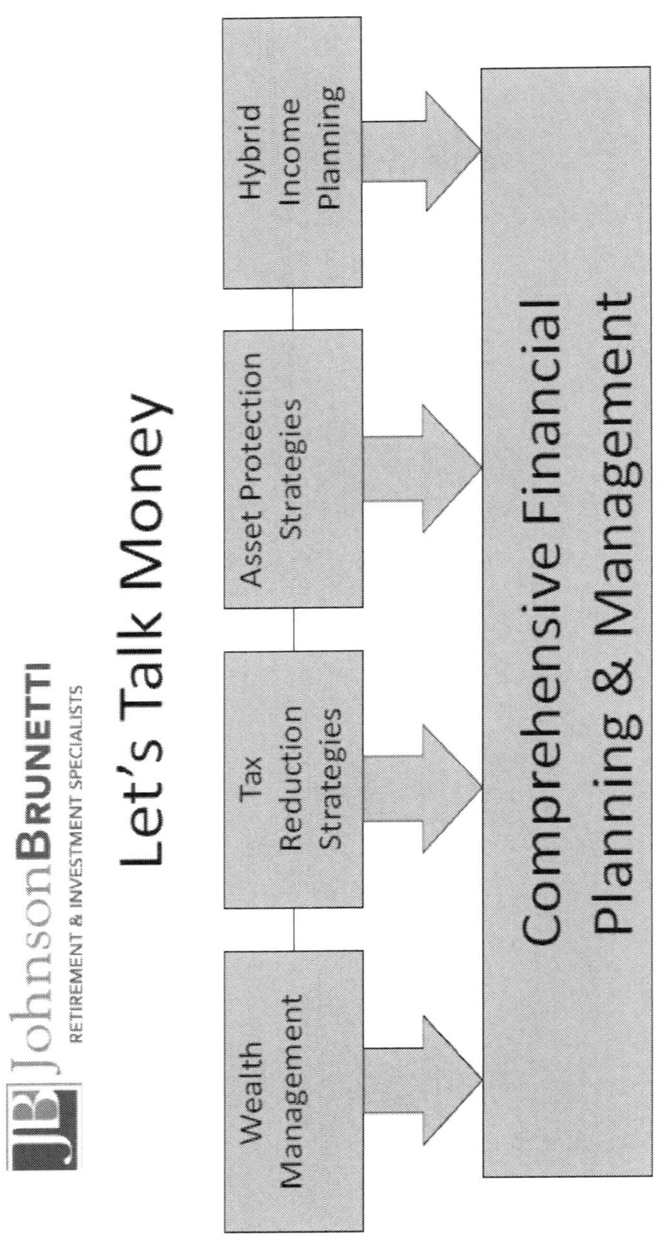

The 4 areas of service we offer our clients.

59126895R00050

Made in the USA
Charleston, SC
28 July 2016